MW01331987

This Notebook Belongs To
